Everybody Poos

Taro Gomi

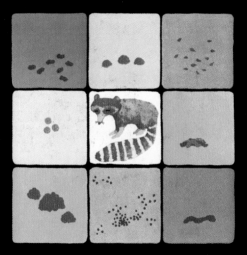

FRANCES LINCOLN
CHILDREN'S BOOKS

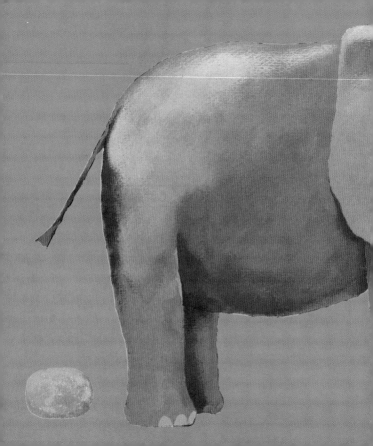

An elephant
makes a
big poo.

A mouse makes
a tiny poo.

A one-hump camel
makes a one-hump poo.

And a two-hump camel
makes a two-hump poo.

Only
joking!

Fish poo.

So do birds.

And bugs too.

Different
animals
make
different
kinds
of poo.

Different
shapes,
different
colours,
even
different
smells.

Which end is the snake's bottom?

What does whale

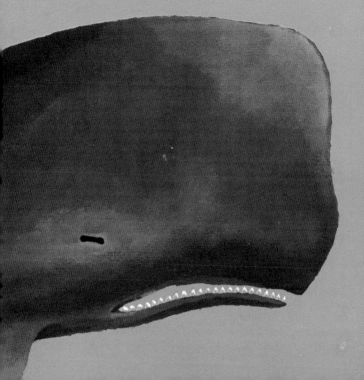

poo look like?

Some stop to poo.

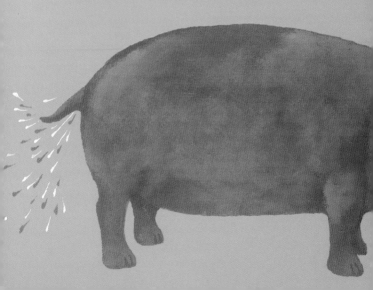

Others do it
on the move.

Some poo here
and there.

Others do it
in a special
place.

Grown-ups poo.

Children poo too.

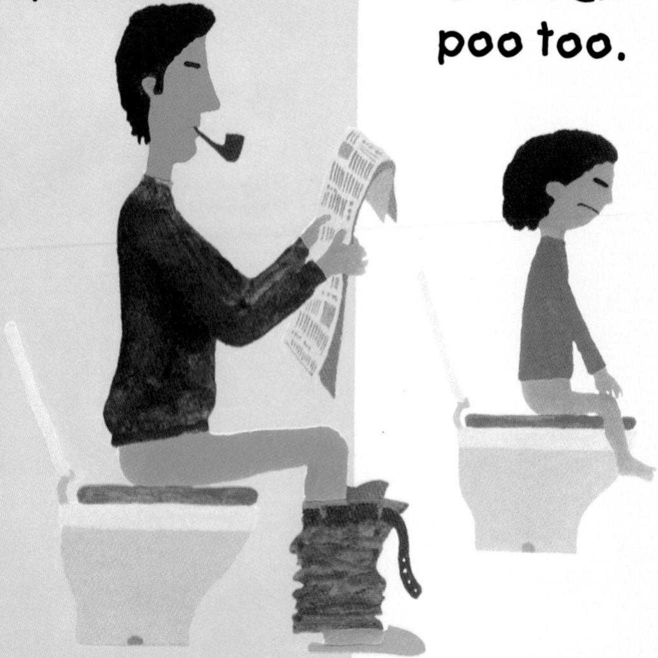

Some children poo on the potty,

others poo in their nappies.

Some animals poo and take no notice.

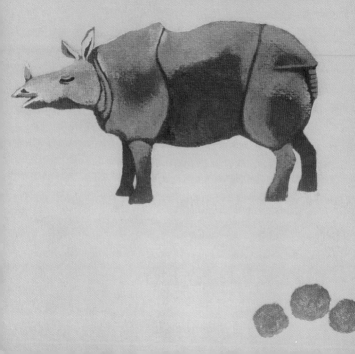

Others clean up
after themselves.

He wipes himself with paper

and flushes it away.

All living things eat, so...

everybody poos.

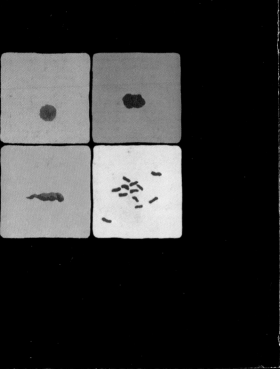